Girlie Calendar

"Song is mysterious. It seems to arise when the separation between sophistication and simplicity has been submerged in deep water. Song is that ringing-out of the wrung heart whereby what is personal becomes what is universal—and so it is fitting that all the archetypal seasons in Mary Meriam's *Girlie Calendar* have their own specific songs to share, their own ardent delights. Yet these delights are hard-fought, because song is also that inspiring moment of transcendence so in evidence in the courage of these lines: *A knife of pain may bend you over double, / but hover, swing from your trapeze, breathe.* Mary Meriam's songs are thus both breath-taking and breath-giving. Indeed, there is a rigor of architecture in these poems, as well as in the construction of the book as a whole, that is exacting, deliberate, astonishingly disciplined—and yet surrendering to such songs, as a reader, seems as natural as breathing. *Let steel become a sigh,* she sings to herself in her month of August. Those five words rise and fall as an exquisitely fragile monument to all song. I would even go so far as to say that they are a powerful medicine for what ails us."

R. Nemo Hill

Girlie Calendar

Poems
2002-2012

Mary Meriam

Headmistress Press
2014

Copyright © 2014 by Mary Meriam
All rights reserved.

ISBN-13: 978-0692216729
ISBN-10: 0692216723

This book may not be reproduced, in whole or in part, including illustrations, in any form (beyond that permitted by Sections 107 and 108 of the U.S. Copyright Law and except by reviewers for the public press), without written permission from the publishers.

Cover Art: "Flora" (1913) by Louise Abbéma (1853–1927)
Oil on canvas, 156.2 cm x 167 cm
Courtesy of Wikipedia Commons, Public Domain

Cover & book design by Mary Meriam.

Published by Headmistress Press
60 Shipview Lane
Sequim, WA 98382
Telephone: 917-428-8312
Email: headmistresspress@gmail.com
Website: headmistresspress.blogspot.com

With deepest gratitude for her
inspiration, friendship, and books,
I dedicate my Girlie Calendar to

Lillian
Faderman

Contents

January
Wu Tsao's Seclusion	3
Sappho in Exile	6
The Lake	7
Bee Bouts-rimés	8
Beginning with a Line by Robert Frost	9
The Loser	10

February
Stationmaster	13
The Boston Soak	14
Valentine	15
To Elizabeth Bishop	16

March
Soup	19
Farewell to my delight	20

April
On the 40th Anniversary of Lillian & Phyllis	23
Prayer for Leaf	24
Trip Triolet Trio	25
My Rhona	26
Facts About Romance	27
Comfort Song	28
Elaine	29

May
I wanted you	33
Birdhouse	34
Hot Spell	35
What We Do	36
Red Kiss	37
Had We But	38

June
Ladies in Waiting	41
What rhymes with breasts?	42
may the women in prison dance	43
Girlhood	44
How Like You This	45
A Garland of Sighs	46
Sonneglige	47
Gaze	48
World	49

July
The Romance of Middle Age	53
Lingua Lesbian	54
Eureka Springs	55
Dance of a Dozen Lovers	56
Workshop Romance	57
Farmer's Market	58

August
I'm still here	61
Seashore	62
Who's this coming out of the sun?	63
Vincent Van Go-Gogh	64
To Be Recited By Sappho On The Fourth Plinth In Trafalgar Square	65
And	66
When I Meet Her By the Seashore	67

September
On the Breakwater	71
The Great God Pollen	72
What will I do?	73
Daylight Losing Time	74

Lone Poem	75
Daylilies	76
Open Sea	78
Beginning to Dance	79
Futile the winds	80

October
Lighthouse Keeper	83
Anchor Hitch	84

November
Time	87
The Loser's Lament	88
Intersection	89
Enough	90
The Need for Reading	91

December
Sonett	95
A Cappella	96
You	97
Notes	98
Acknowledgments	99

January

All January wanted was a home,
and not these crows, and not these frozen trees,
limbful of snow. It was a home, with these:
a door to close, a chest of drawers, a comb.

Wu Tsao's Seclusion

January 16
my toes touch the soft edge
of my new mattress
soft as the bare breast of a lover
soft as the rainfall tonight
patting and tapping the sodden ground

and the memory of her scent arousing
and blinding me lingers decades later
like a satsuma tangerine's
sweet-sour soaking of my mouth

February 1
chance of snow tonight
will we get out tomorrow
to pick up the mail?

February 7
it's Saturday night
I'm too busy having fun
no time for haikus

February 14
the supermarket check-out clerk's
warm ready smile
penetrates my sore mood,
fluorescent lights, my failures

"I remember you don't need receipts,"
she says, showing it, taking it back,
and laughing playfully

I smile and let my good wishes wash
all over her, her feet standing for hours,
and all the troubles found
in supermarket check-out jobs
for older married ladies

February 23
February ends
clouds gray
black cows and cow pies dot the fields
skunks and cats dead
roadside decoration
sixty miles I drive
a narrow path through farms and hills
three horses munch whatever's left
hawks, eagles, crows, vultures prey
my winter mind
wakes up in town today
when walking down the empty aisle
she approaches me
with eyes that speak my language
richly colored eyes that gaze directly
into mine and laugh
later, by chance, our eyes meet again
and sing and dance

March 29
ah, middle age,
I have arrived at your empty castle
the guards have taken me away
my face no longer fresh enough for spring
that hits my mind with wind and rain
and sweet delicate pastel little flowers

instant everywhere
your crime lives on unknown
you only know that one by one
the ones you love are gone
and she took herself away
so why should I care
I will not allow myself to ask
but I will remain silent
and listen to the chirping birds

Sappho in Exile

How would I know the city? By
a thousand cuts or one hello,
her dress of black or bad goodbye.

One sparrow from a tree would fly.
The traffic on the streets would flow.
How would I know the city? By

her look, the question in her eye,
her faith in false Pinocchio,
her dress of black or bad goodbye.

I love her still, don't ask me why.
Like others then, she had to go.
How would I know the city? By

the shock, the press, the loss of I,
the library, the picture show,
her dress of black or bad goodbye,

her hand reposing on her thigh,
her lion's paw of lasting woe.
How would I know the city? By
her dress of black, her bad goodbye.

The Lake

Suzanne, poetic fauna blues the lake,
forest full moon fish who cruise the lake.

What do I know in my van winkle world?
My old binoculars peruse the lake.

The past came back and bit me in the ass,
monstrosity who would abuse the lake.

The present drags me under every day.
The Osage homeless ghost tattoos the lake.

She was a poet and she killed herself.
What can I do about the bruise? The lake.

Promise to soothe the hurt and never hurt,
calling myself to task. The muse, the lake.

Unlock the throat, unlock the mind, and sing,
sing for the tongue-tied girls who lose the lake.

This merry lass an everblooming dreamer,
praying these ghazal waves transfuse the lake.

Bee Bouts-rimés

Today I wore my face called undepressed.
Tomorrow I'll put on my face of rain.
This switch of faces is a constant strain
but such is life, a queen bee's busy nest.
Some days I feel that God has knelt and blest
my bees, and other days God wraps a chain
around my wings that reaches to my brain.
When can I sleep, God, when can I rest?
Day after day I smell the stinky blast
of gardens wearing faces in a wilt.
God's coming back to save us any day.
Today I wander through the beehive built
of all the dregs I saved from my bee past,
my God face hidden in the eggs I lay.

Beginning with a Line by Robert Frost

They spoke to the fugitive in my heart as if it were leaf to leaf.
They spoke to me one windy day from the copse nearby my house.
Low in the night they rustled to thief and owl and addict and mouse.
Let me be deaf to the crash of trouble and the mighty underworld.
The pile of rotten branches and gold leaves lies there dead and swirled.
It would take every court in the countryside to count the fallen leaves.
The judges must number themselves among the dirt-thirsty thieves.
I live in a room of cold-toed winter glowing with no relief.
Wandering silent, muttered about, I move from grief to grief.

The Loser

I lost Aunt Peggy's silver ring.
I lost my sister's golden chain.
It seems like I lose everything.
I lost Aunt Peggy's silver ring.
If you should have a gift to bring,
be careful of my slippery drain:
I lost Aunt Peggy's silver ring;
I lost my sister's golden chain;
I lost the song I meant to sing.

February

Make me the heart of February, please,
her sweet and frilly be-mine valentine,
shot through and through with love incarnadine
and holy scented essence of heart's ease.

Stationmaster

The clatter of the world goes by
and pulls along each passing day.
You search for light along the way
and long for someone standing by
to put the shame to every lie
and explicate the shades of gray
as, clattering, the world goes by
and pulls along each passing day.
You feel your every heartbeat sigh
with grief you cannot chase away
with friends who only can betray
with flowers that will always die,
as, clattering, the world goes by
and pulls along each passing day.

The Boston Soak

She shovels the snow from her drive
then takes her Sunday bath.
What does she know that I don't know?
she wonders in her long soaking bath.
She does make me laugh.
How far would I have to drive?
She splashes and slides in her bath
forgetting what she knows or doesn't know.
Her own skin belongs to her
and hot bubbles, there is no drive,
it's only love, and love is like water
unencumbered by "he" or "she."
One last slosh of soaked loofah,
and she steps out of the bath.
Down the drain goes the water,
where it ends, she doesn't know.
Perhaps in the snow on her drive.

Valentine

I love you very much.
Come keep me company
Tonight in fantasy
Because we cannot touch.

This word you close your eyes.
This line my lips on yours.
This rhyme the heartbeat soars.
This stanza moans and sighs.

This verse is incomplete,
My images run dry,
Because the pronouns I
And you have yet to meet.

To Elizabeth Bishop

We were standing in the dim living room of a stranger
Night was upon us and you were to die the next year

You were small and your hand was small in my hand
Even if we had spoken, I only remember silence

We had both suffered in our separate lives
The pulse of your hand in my hand is alive

The suffering was immense in the room
We shared only silence and one touch

My lover was eager to introduce us
Yes, we were looking at each other

March

On windy nights in March, her stars align,
like satin stitches neatly placed in rows,
and for a moment, though the rough wind blows,
her needlepoint is part of the design.

Soup

spinach: I was sound asleep, so I guess the tornadoes passed me by
asparagus: snow flurries this morning, drove to bank anyway
garlic: banker forgot his notary stamp
shallots: drove banker to get his stamp
leeks: banker said mouse was running around the parking lot
corn: upset about the snow
carrots: no accumulation
celery: mailbox empty this morning
potatoes: both glad and sad
cabbage: washed dishes, watched moon rise
butter: wondered why moon had missing piece
bean stock: heard on radio moon eclipsed tonight
salt: forecast says 62 on Monday
pepper: thought you should know

Farewell to my delight

Yes, I could cling like honeysuckle vine,
except that half of love is letting go,
and doesn't pruning help the flowers grow,
and after all, I cannot call you mine.

Yes, like a baby, I could cry and whine,
except that childhood ended long ago,
and isn't comfort something I should know,
and after all, you've clearly drawn the line.

So I will say farewell to my delight,
the sun, the moon, the rain, the snow, the sky,
and all the plants and creatures of the earth,
and I will close the door and call this night,
and call myself a child who says goodbye
and sleeps away the grief for all she's worth.

April

When April weeps, the tears drip on her toes,
the water rises in the jade-stone lake,
a blue jay shakes the red-bud blooms awake,
in rainy light, the green grass rosy glows.

On the 40th Anniversary of Lillian & Phyllis

If one could read the poem of a face,
then I've read yours and memorized the words.
Two lips for wit and bliss would be the case,
if one could read the poem of your face.
An honest ear, a tooth for truth, for grace,
two flirting eyes that flit like little birds.
If one could read the poem of a face,
then I've read yours and memorized the words.

Prayer for Leaf

The last old leaves have blown away,
and I'm alone, undressed, and lost,
shivering in a new spring breeze
beside the lake that laps the shore.

Blossom me slowly, bloom me good,
and draw my fancy flowers nigh.
Maple me softly, oak me strong,
and let my close-green clothing grow.

Trip Triolet Trio

1.
I have to go pick up the mail,
and then make breakfast, lunch, and dinner,
then go to sleep, then without fail,
I have to go pick up the mail.
I won't have time to tell my tale.
At least I am a well-fed sinner.
Now I must go pick up the mail,
and then make breakfast, lunch, and dinner.

2.
Ah bella Maria, the barber is singing,
the barber is snipping, the barber is dancing,
the barber is trimming, the phone is ringing,
ah bella Maria, the barber is singing,
the barber is humming, the barber is flinging
steamed green beans, the barber's romancing,
ah bella Maria, the barber is singing,
the barber is snipping, the barber is dancing.

3.
I cross from Missouri to Arkansas
on Fridays to shop in town, tra la.
With turtles and vultures and crows, caw-caw,
I cross from Missouri to Arkansas.
The sound of these states is stuck in my craw.
I'm stuck in the states of blah and blah.
I cross from Missouri to Arkansas
on Fridays to shop in town, tra la.

My Rhona

Ah yes, I scrutinized *The Art of Meeting
Women,* and fell for Rhona Sacks, her eyes,
her friendly smile, her hand held out in greeting,
her quick chit-chat. My Rhona is so wise!
I'd like to ask her, "Hey, what happens if
I'm not afraid, I'm not a slob, I say
hello, I'm cheery, kind, and not too stiff,
but she just doesn't care?" "Well then, don't stay,"
my Rhona pithily advises, "Move."
Helpfully, my Rhona urges lots
of get up, go, and find another groove.
"And if I'm stuck in her hard-hearted plots?"
"Break free," my Rhona counsels, "and be true
to the Rhona that I introduced you to."

Facts About Romance

The neighbor's cat is here again.
A heron bombs the silver blooms.
Moonrise lights the soggy tombs.
I go to sleep, wake up, and then,
who can tell me why or when,
creeping by the witchy brooms,
the neighbor's cat is here again.
A heron bombs the silver blooms.
Swear and sign it with a pen!
Follow her, the verdict looms.
Rush her from the rising rooms,
the bed of lavender, the wren.
The neighbor's cat is here again.

Comfort Song

In the town
She heals with words,
She wears a gown
Of berry birds.

In the city
She flies around,
She dons a pretty
Breeze she found.

How I miss
Her leafy park
And tulip kiss
In my cold dark.

Elaine

Elaine! I loved your face, your hands, your voice,
your touch, your mouth, your teeth, your toss
of light sweet aching hair,
the winding way you came across
the river to my bed. Our small-town fame
grew long along the muddy Delaware,
then we were swept away, our slant affair
not strong enough to swim against the tide
but stuck in narrow straits and forced to hide,
till you, Elaine, left me alone,
unknown.

May

The life they tell of May is a mistake.
They simply wanted her to love a man
she didn't. Skewed her voice to fit their plan.
Left May alone with her peculiar ache.

I wanted you

I wanted you. Instead, I got the moon.
Who wouldn't stop her rising? Not the moon.

Put collard greens in noodle casserole,
spring onions, chard, and stir the pot, the moon.

Rain, rain, refrigerator, shower, thunder,
blood summer patio—how hot the moon.

The little virgin forest, thickets, leaves,
a locket round the lake, my cot, the moon.

Who tugs her sacred through the sky, the night?
Who rings the bell, but who forgot the moon?

Like mares in May that thud the thorny ground,
I'm sleeveless in the lover plot, the moon.

Birdhouse

Why do my bluebirds choose the spring to leave?
The greening grass insults my nest of loss.
The pecks of pain they left behind do grieve
My very grove. Some memories of moss
I'll keep, for eggs. I know the old routine,
The way the bluebirds come and go. The wing,
Bright blue, the breast, a shade of tangerine,
Belie, alas, the cheep-cheep song they sing.

Hot Spell

This sonnet holds the hope of something hot:
a summer night with soft cicada din,
a sultry rush of fingers on the skin,
a tender lightning bolt that hits the spot.

Or in the city, ripe with heat and rot,
a staircase to a loft where we begin
a strip-down to the hardest core within,
a culture shock, the climax of the plot.

This sonnet drops my hand and doesn't care
that here I lie alone, again, in bed,
the chilly springtime flooding me with pain.
As if I need the sonnet to explain
a couplet rhymes, a couplet is a pair,
my sweat is rain, the heat is in my head.

What We Do

She swallows whole the sun and moon
    and eats my tiny star,
I lead her to my lonely room
    to see what day we are.

Her cosmic arms envelop me,
    her gamma rays caress,
Her hair uncurls my twisted key,
    her seabird screeches yes.

She calls me summer blossom time,
    I call her darling snow,
She sucks me like a lemon-lime
    while icy billows blow.

Red Kiss

Who will miss me when I'm dead?
Maybe someone reading this
is just the sort of daisy head
who will miss me when I'm dead
and planted in a tulip bed.
To her, I offer this red kiss.
Who will miss me when I'm dead?
Maybe someone reading this.

Had We But

The fantasy of me and you in bed—
iambic lines the couplet screw in bed.

Suppose you walk me to the SoHo stop,
drawn to the thought of someone new in bed?

You ride me on your motorbike in Portsmouth—
Charybdis close, a dirty blue in bed.

The common moon in darklit summer bliss,
deserted field the French taboo in bed.

I didn't wake you for the falling stars—
how could I know what you would do in bed?

I sketch you naked sleeping in first light,
the memory of nights for two in bed.

Some airy breaths I bring you here to see—
you bring me here, long overdue in bed.

June

Where is the girl of June who skipped and ran
along the feather lane of birdy hill?
I'd like to give her my last daffodil.
She's lost on river road where she began.

Ladies in Waiting

Again, the ladies in the store,
standing behind me with a smile,
will wait but want a little more.

They want to chat, perhaps explore
my fuzzy cobalt jacket pile.
Again, the ladies in the store

will want to pat my shoulder or,
enchanted by my T-shirt style,
will wait but want a little more,

will slip their fingers past the door
to check the label. Versatile!
Again, the ladies in the store

will add amusement to the chore
of shopping up and down the aisle,
will wait but want a little more

of me, it seems, and my rapport.
I'll wait with them a little while.
Again, the ladies in the store
will wait but want a little more.

What rhymes with breasts?

It's good to know what rhymes with breasts
I wish I'd never seen your breasts

You never know when lines will dance
In girlie pictures in your book

The pirouette of words suggests
My longing for you never rests

It's good to know what rhymes with breasts
I wish I'd never seen your breasts!

While cruising on poetic quests
But it's too late for weak protests

While balancing on cliffs and chance
You stripped. I burned. You gave. I took.

It's good to know what rhymes with breasts
I wish I'd never seen your breasts

You never know when lines will dance
In girlie pictures in your book

may the women in prison dance

women dance, your dresses of purple linen
swaying, dance on flowering grasses, sunlight
dancing too on brown skin and silver bracelets
        you are invited

ice cold water, clean and refreshing, drink it
lunch is ready, feast on the grapes you gathered,
ripe and juicy, sunflower seeds and almonds,
        roasted and crunchy

lovely island, dreaming of lesbos, scented
seaside song, her laughter is pleasure, shadows
lead the way to late afternoon and making
        love with your lover

Girlhood

In my girlhood
I did my time under a gray
sweatshirt hood.

In a crazy way
I was always alone
in bad neighborhoods.

I used a pay phone
to call my womanhood.
No answer—no good.

Inside I'm this way:
hooded, good,
off the hook.

How Like You This

Lily, dear heart, how like you this,
the sailing of some sweet perfume
and in its wake her salty kiss?

Blithely skirting the abyss,
you climb the staircase to her room.
Lily, dear heart, how like you this,

the summer's fading roar and hiss,
the cool clean cot, the steady zoom,
and in its wake her salty kiss?

Lip to lip, you cannot miss
the minute parsing of her bloom.
Lily, dear heart, how like you this,

the study of a woman's bliss,
the stripping of her prison gloom,
and in its wake her salty kiss?

She studies so as not to miss
the sight of Lily at her loom.
Lily, dear heart, how like you this,
and in its wake her salty kiss?

A Garland of Sighs

A cat?
or moaning cow?
or loon booming the lake?
Some creature howls away our hushed
        hello.
Pleasure
the piney woods
rustles my leafy dreams.
I sleep in shadow bright stained glass
        without her.
Should I
arrange the sheet
around my slumbering
in case the shrieking leaping sheep
        feel shy?
I lost
the key of C
but she was there in spirit
the sharpest note of ecstasy
        was shared.
A car
veers off the street
strikes like a bowling ball.
Manhattan held her shroud and kissed
        her mouth.
A cat
the piney woods
around my slumbering
the sharpest note of ecstasy
        her mouth.

Sonneglige

O négligée neglected far too long.
O fantasies.
O dust. O right and wrong.
O season of heat. O freeze.

Gaze

And oh the amazonian old girl,
her polo collar straight up, and her eyes
averted from the inner-outer whirl
of actions indisputably unwise.
Administration, I believe? So clean,
her clothes, so crisp. An early seventies
collegiate scene, we cross the campus green,
and as we pass, I see her skin say *please*.
I'm sorry there's no language round her lips.
Her walking on suggests that she'd prefer
to stay alone. Now fearful winter tips
my fancy back in time, I fancy her,
the model of restraint, the employee,
who'd never touch young lesbians like me.

World

Anyone could, for love, traverse the world.
Cally sings to trees, disperse the world.

She bikes through forests in a foreign land,
winter, summer, empty purse, the world.

The jet plane lifts and lowers, glints of steel.
The four winds faster, harder, curse the world.

When moss and violets line the rocky creeks,
when all that flows is breaking, verse the world.

Flying or stopping still to pen the page,
having for better or for worse, the world.

My simple summary, my gift to Cally:
there is a good that will reverse the world.

July

July, come find me in the fish's gill.
July, come splash and tip my quick canoe.
July, come whisper who is kind and true.
July, come when you willow, if you will.

The Romance of Middle Age

Now that I'm fifty, let me take my showers
at night, no light, eyes closed. And let me swim
in cover-ups. My skin's tattooed with hours
and days and decades, head to foot, and slim
is just a faded photograph. It's strange
how people look away who once would look.
I didn't know I'd undergo this change
and be the unseen cover of a book
whose plot, though swift, just keeps on getting thicker.
One reaches for the pleasures of the mind
and heart to counteract the loss of quicker
knowledge. One feels old urgencies unwind,
although I still pluck chin hairs with a tweezer,
in case I might attract another geezer.

Lingua Lesbian

The summer English is forbidden,
we have no words to share,
and so a language that was hidden
finds the open air.

Her curls of silky sunny light,
blond blooming in my hand,
entangle me and turn the night
gentle where we stand.

Her Russian babbles in my ear,
mon français sways her hips,
we laugh, go quiet, I draw near
and kiss her rosy lips.

Eureka Springs

The farmer's market in the little Arkansas tourist town, each farmer's tarp tight over a table at the butt-end of a pick-up; and the strawberry farmer in the spring, now the potato farmer in the hotter months, his old face pockmarked and mealy, his teeth large and brown; the farmer from France, with the most popular organic produce, his sensuous accent surreal among the flat patois of the mountain folk, his buttery lettuce light, crisp, tender; Bunny, with her carrots and New England roots, her garlic first green, then moist, pearly cloves, with her bright bags of kale and chard, her bent fingers, her hunger and faded memories; the sky hot baked blue, or dove gray heavy with rain; the banjo player and his spoon-playing wife; the lines of children's drawings in primary colors and puffs of wind.

Dance of a Dozen Lovers

April holds the hands of May,
kissing her tender palms and fingers.
Before the blooms of June hold sway,
April holds the hands of May.
Before July brings her bouquet,
before her lover, August, lingers,
April holds the hands of May,
kissing her tender palms and fingers.

October wanders through the rain,
looking for leaves September left.
Shivering past the window pane,
October wanders through the rain.
Spinning November's weather vane,
December fools; and still bereft,
October wanders through the rain,
looking for leaves September left.

Midnight, the lovers turn in sleep,
in separate months and separate beds,
while January makes the leap.
Midnight, the lovers turn in sleep,
while February slides her sleds
to meet her March. And yet, they weep.
Midnight, the lovers turn in sleep,
in separate months and separate beds.

Workshop Romance

I like your verb, I like your noun,
I like how you've got grammar down,
I like the way you get work done,
I like the prizes you have won,
but, darling, can we paint the town,

and will you wear a cosmic crown,
and spangly satin crimson gown
of sheer, resplendent golden sun?
I like your verb, I like your noun,

I like your stature and renown,
I like your smile, I like your frown,
but, darling, must you always shun
my adjectives? Are you a nun?
Am I a silly, sorry clown?
I like your verb! I like your noun!

Farmer's Market

watermelon: I was pretty once in an androgynous way
zucchini: now I am too old to be looked at by anyone
carrots: man or woman
cantaloupe: I shall not reveal my name or age
okra: if you saw me at the farmer's market
tomatoes: I would not be standing behind a table
onions: laden with tomatoes, onions
garlic: I would be carrying brown paper bags
yellow squash: filling them up
basil: I would not be the teenage boy
scallions: holding his father's arm
lettuce: legs strangely twisted
string beans: who walks with more vertical than horizontal
beets: movement, as if each step requires
eggplant: a leap into the air and the most intense concentration
radish: I am able to climb the staircase two steps at a time
sweet pepper: and climb the staircase seventy times
peaches: until sweat drips like blood
blackberries: my legs marble pillars
turnip: my vanity strong as my marble legs so that
parsley: I quickly forget the boy's twisted legs
cucumber: and his pain

August

Downstream in August, down the heron flew,
straight through the secret bower where we stay
in ferny waterfalls, safe from the day,
forgotten as her words, *a fonds perdu.*

I'm still here

I'm still here holding up the sky for you,
bawling this heart-to-heart goodbye for you.

I'm still the child who cooks the stony stew,
the chickadee who learned to fly for you.

She looks so rich, her face so fresh and new—
you're more than friends, I catch her sigh for you.

Do I sound bitter? Am I green or blue?
Don't leave again! Don't make me cry for you!

I send some poems to the *Screw Review*,
I sit around and wait and die for you.

The marvel of my muse is constant, true.
With dedicated lust, I try for you.

Seashore

Walking the shore alone on cliffs or sand,
the constant senseless waves a steady thrum
(the planet's blood, or mine), the wind at hand,
tangling my thoughts. Where does the wind come from?
They bring me here each summer, to the coast.
Aunt Peggy married wealth, but now it's lost.
She belts a number to the Holy Ghost,
her spirit one with His and damn the cost.
The shades of English novels haunt my mind,
as on the shore, a handsome boy walks by
then stops. Is this the shell I meant to find?
I'm still too young to penetrate the lie,
but I will turn away from boys and home,
and trade my seashells for the mermaid's comb.

Who's this coming out of the sun?

Oh baby you hot hot mama. You hot virgin island at noon summertime. Lizard crawl the wall. Old queen lay by the cove watch wavelets roll. Dew by the light of the sun coming up, come your greenery glittering. Open your tent flap, my little scorpion, bite me, bite me. Drink it down, coconut milk. Baby you hot beauty coming out of the sun you swallow me honeydew. Let me scream a little fuck for you, hm, all right, lay down your bright beam glory here fruit flesh. Come from the sun ray sting me.

Vincent Van Go-Gogh

Again it starts, the solid wall of rain,
good for the farmers, good for cows and cash.
Again it stabs, the rolling pin of pain,
the itch, the broken bone, the tender rash,
the worn-out tooth and eye, the final crash.
We pause to listen to the thunder fart,
as lightning's tongue delivers one more lash.
The earth is tearing up my heart, my heart
a pastry on a shelf, a baker's tart.
Again I brush the silence on in blue,
they could be rising crows, but this my art
repairs the yellow clock I left with you.
I left it on the chair beside the bed,
telling the time, rewinding in my head.

To Be Recited By Sappho On The Fourth Plinth In Trafalgar Square

Father Sky, you droop like a used umbrella.
Passersby, attend to this gallant beauty.
Gone, your pigeon riches, no mouldy droppings
pattern the pavement.

Here my holler rings off the stately towers,
bound for Britain's crown. And resounding sweet as
countertenor solos, my vocalizing
douses the globe with

falcons, fountains, blue-crested wenches, lions.
London heart, I measure your pathways always,
perched pontificating, my arms embracing
skylines and honour.

And

Through summer scorch, be like the trees, breathe,
and through the winter's cracking freeze, breathe.

You gather fragments scratched on broken glass,
and poets drowned in seven seas breathe.

You find her locked inside, you open doors,
you lift her off her buckled knees, breathe.

A knife of pain may bend you over double,
but hover, swing from your trapeze, breathe.

You grip your breath too tight, now let it fly
free from its cage, and like the bees, breathe.

Marry your lungs and air, let steel become
a sigh, be like a leafy breeze, breathe.

When I Meet Her By the Seashore

I shall
untwine her time
unravel her travel
undo her mood
unfasten her battens
unmesh her dress
unbutton her bubbles
unleash her fresh.

And then I shall
unwind her behind
uncouple her trouble
unearth her worth
unstaple her paper
unzip her yip
unbuckle her tickle
untuck her lush.

September

September's kohl-rimmed eyes at cabaret,
her turtleneck in black, the color wrong.
But will she listen? No, this is her song,
the little room now falling, flows away.

On the Breakwater

One summer night, when wispy moon had set,
and slothful sea lay tranquil, lapping shore,
and stars glittered, the two young women met
and walked with fingertips in touch, unsure
of where to go, and found a place to sit,
remote, and turned their backs on lights and town
to gaze, without a word, at darkness lit,
but hardly, by a thin gold line thrown down
by Venus, with no sound except the sigh
and suck of ripples, and an owl's high shrill
screeching, at times, from hillside trees nearby.
Then one locked arms around her friend, until
she felt the fervor of her clasp could be
in rhythm with the stealthily heaving sea.

The Great God Pollen

The Great God Pollen comes to earth in fall
with golden promise, I suppose, to plant
some seeds, to grow some trees, to have a ball
with Goddess Wind, I guess. But no, I can't
rejoice in this romance, because my nose
is dripping, eyes are tearing, throat is sore,
and warm and sunny golden days are those
that bring Lord Pollen and his paramour
the closest to destroying inner peace:
I'm in a fury! Pouting, sullen, crying,
because the summer's gone, because the geese
come down from Canada, because they're flying
with Goddess Wind and Great God Pollen. Pity,
I doubt that I'll survive outside the city.

What will I do?

The answer is a room.
There is a bed.

The bed is there for me to lie on.
I go there

yellow leaves already falling
for the sake of lust

though I must
imagine

"you"
my body creaks closes opens moans moves

as it has
other afternoons.

Daylight Losing Time

I dread turning clocks back an hour.
I'm scared of the turning of leaves.
I'm sorry my mood turns so sour.
I dread turning clocks back an hour.
Can I spring up ahead like a flower?
In fall my clock withers and grieves.
I dread turning clocks back an hour.
I'm scared of the turning of leaves.

Lone Poem

Manhattan. Early eighties. Marilyn
is in, in word, in mind, in bed, in air
I barely breathe, invisible, in skin,
as if this is our lesbian affair.
Instead, she's rising as I crack and sink
and roam to Womanbooks, as if to save
Madwoman in the Attic. Dusk like drink
on sidewalks back, four punkheads misbehave.
One grabs my crotch, for what, for laughs? forget
they could have raped me there in Central Park,
for I was mad and cursed their sorry threat
with lip, with will to live, like wild tree bark
on thick and stately trees I wander under,
lost in the star that tore my heart asunder.

Daylilies

Monday
I phone my soul on Monday, fervent girl,
while leafy shadow puppets sway the curtain.
She gives my bednight bliss a deepsweet swirl.
My little moon loves me, of this I'm certain.

Tuesday
In Crooked Crowville, Tuesday's name is fire.
For her, I take the stand to testify
about the furtive spring of my desire
and how I swallow burning sky and sigh.

Wednesday
Slow goddess, may I fondle Wednesday's ass
and screw her bones into the stratosphere?
Slow goddess hands me water in a glass
and answers very slowly, "Not yet, dear."

Thursday
What quiet Thursday knew, she knew by thunder:
the farmer's hand that cupped her written face,
the poet's papers tossed when she goes under,
the table's wooden legs, the pencil case.

Friday
The weight is all on Friday, oh, what must
she do? Silkslip the sticky golden ring,
flashing the flaxen honeymoon of lust,
upon the bluewing of gamete King Ing?

Saturday
"I know a way," says Saturday, "to lay
a dame: obtain a title, trade, or fame."
This wisdom is dispensed on washing day
to peasants making hay in mortal shame.

Sunday
She is the deep, the gleam, the Sunday dance
I dreamed about. She is the shell, the feather,
the leaf I found, when walking about, by chance.
She makes the lilies bright in rainy weather.

Open Sea

Do you ever rendezvous?
Would you meet me in the mist,
the harbor mist, just me and you?
Or do you never rendezvous;
the thought itself is too taboo.
The literary term is tryst,
if you never rendezvous.
But would you meet me in the mist?

Beginning to Dance

Slow sweet music plays and she
Begins to move her hands as we
O yes she whispers this could be
The granite limits passing me
O wrap me round and quarry me
She swims my waters deep and she
Splash she nestles closer dear
Grove she whispers in my ear
The hazel green trees rustling near

Futile the winds

I close my eyes to go to sleep
and search the velvet night
for any comfort I can keep
or any dream invite.

And then I wonder where you are
and if I could be there,
closer to you, or not so far,
or more than just a prayer.

One word is like a world to me.
Please show me how to reach
the other side of fantasy,
the providence of speech.

Serious night, all undone,
and dark more elemental,
there an answer, there is none,
nor kiss, nor kind, nor gentle.

October

I do adore October's blue sarong,
the sliding slits along her whistling hips,
and I would die to kiss her ruby lips
for all the wet and rotting leaf night long.

Lighthouse Keeper

O pitiless mirror
space empty, smile
tested, trite.
I look for a sign,
you ruthlessly reflect
your slick glass
glued to a dusty off-white
bathroom wall. I'll take
your quick dark ride.

O mattress-mistress,
into you I press
draped with duvet
to every curve.
Flat, inert, hard
you take touch here, there,
then listen to my
then ease my down dark
slope to sleep.

O treasure, lover
naked sleeping
in my tiny room
I draw dawn points
your hands the cello.
Years later I
struggle to remember
kiss, voice, first,
please don't be over.

Anchor Hitch

How do I untie the knot of you?
The poets are professors with degrees!
So much to teach! But I am old and blue.
I lag. I drag behind. I stare at trees,
all woven tight with you for decades now,
cooking and cleaning, mending, keeping house,
wondering what my stringent Fates allow.
They bellow belowdecks and make me grouse.
Their white robes billow on a fancy yacht
on oceans I may never see; and yet,
I am well-fed and comfortable, and not
the waif I was. So why be so upset?
Because the goddess of my dreams is where
I'm not. *Fates, let me go! oh wreck me there!*

November

November steels herself for this eclipse.
She twirls her silver ring, light wheels to dark.
Shuffle around the closed amusement park.
Take flight before the skygray canvas rips.

Time

Why did you leave me all alone this time,
a bitter Himalayan zone this time?

I found the spices dug in Shakespeare's forest.
(Here exeunt players with a groan this time.)

My tears were buried by bedraggled squirrels,
leaping from limb to limb, bemoan this time.

Gold leaves of words were falling helplessly,
your silence ivy overgrown this time.

How was I supposed to curl on nothing?
It was the hardest coldest stone this time.

Sword branches tore my cope on Halloween,
red berry for the bird unknown this time.

I weave together lachrymary lines,
a cloth for you. I am your own this time.

The Loser's Lament

The winning wealthy poets, photographed
by Avedon, will fly between their homes,
collecting prizes, teaching classes, staffed
with personal assistants, stuffed with poems
that dribble from their mouths and land in books
that stock the superstores, the most elite
of schools, and shelves of readers with the looks
to share their beds and take a dinner seat.

But I'm a poet of a single table.
I wash my dishes at the kitchen sink.
I have nowhere to go, and so I think
I'll sit and write a poem at the table.
The price I pay for every line I write
is measured by the gods in bloody light.

Intersection

Judith and Olga
kiss at the red
light two lips touch

mommy grunts
tut-tut two lips
twisted wreckage

sixties spring
the flash of red tulips
signals go

so I go
leap from no
into knowing

Enough

Lover, take this burden, fling my name,
lullaby your baby, sing my name.

A pretty hamlet free from ghosts and worry,
no wounded names foreshadowing my name.

My bitter legacy runs barefoot down the road.
The bees of bothered beehives sting my name.

Fame is such an aphrodisiac—
come on, come on, come on, sweet, bling my name.

We'll wake up marvelling that we're together.
You'll say, like it means everything, my name.

The Need for Reading

Your words, your birds, the wish that fills my hands,
thunderous words, bright feathers, flapping birds,
migrate inside me from your thoughtful lands.
How could I live without your birdy words?
They pierce my muffled house with mating calls,
they read themselves in silence late at night,
they are the years that fade away, the walls
of years I climb to reach you in the light
where I can read your words again. You lay
your words in rows of opals, rubies, pearls,
for me to read but never touch. You play
my senses with an overture that twirls
my wits like ballerinas. In your book
of words, you satisfy my every look.

December

Outside December's window howls the bark
rolled endlessly, big ocean's opal foam,
then silence. Then she thinks of her shalom,
then longs for home, then hears the morning lark.

Sonett

Perhaps it's time for me to hide away
And cry without a sound, my head sunk low,
Then dry my weary eyes again that oh
Have never, never had a restful day—

And let my glances wander fitfully
Off in the gray, the distant atmosphere,
Pursuing phantom fortune, here and here,
Sick from the constant scramble hurting me—

Or is it time to fling myself straight down
In desperation, let my wildness show
In flaming eyes, the gutter of the town

My turf to growl and pant and puff and frown—
Or is it time for me to simply drown
And cry without a sound, my head sunk low.

(after Fradel Shtok's "Sonett")

A Cappella

You take me to the Swan Hotel for drinks,
the Bach cantata still between us, mute.
When you conduct, your hands make slender links
between us: sing crescendo, sing pursuit.

A tiny table sits between us, still,
encircled by a barroom full of noise.
I'm just eighteen, a secret Sapphic thrill
before me: kiss the girls, forget the boys.

You drive me home along the river curve,
the countryside asleep except for light
from dashboard dials, a single flickering nerve
between us: a cappella, ah the night
will hide the way you shift the gears from choir
to this first touch, our holy duet of desire.

You

The night I was entwined in trees,
I tasted you, my tongue alert.
The deer, pathetic in the freeze,
still leapt away, their feelings hurt,
the forest tight. My dreary crumbs
were eaten, but I tasted there,
as if I knew your dainty plums,
the you that isn't only air.

Notes

"Wu Tsao's Seclusion" – Wu Tsao was an early-nineteenth-century Chinese poet. She was unhappily married, wrote erotic poems to courtesans, had women friends and lovers, and spent her last years in seclusion as a Taoist priestess. sappho.com/poetry/wu_tsao.html

"Bee Bouts-rimés" – From Wordsworth's sonnet "Hark! 'tis the Thrush, undaunted, undeprest."

"The Lake" – Dedicated to Suzanne J. Doyle.

"To Elizabeth Bishop" – The last line is from Muriel Rukeyser's poem "Looking at Each Other."

"How Like You This" – "Dear heart, how like you this?" is from Sir Thomas Wyatt's poem "They Flee From Me."

"Sonneglige" – The title is a form invented by Kathrine Varnes which she describes as "a negligent sonnet, that many poets might not even call a sonnet, but one that flirts with a past life, one with a studied disorder."

"Who's this coming out of the sun" – The title is from "Under Milk Wood" by Dylan Thomas.

"On the Breakwater" – Based on the 1934 short story "Two Hanged Women" by Henry Handel Richardson.

"Sonett" – Thanks to Lillian Faderman's help, I translated this sonnet. Fradel Shtok was one of the earliest modern Yiddish women writers to gain recognition for her work, and one of the first Yiddish poets to write sonnets.

Acknowledgments

My thanks to the editors of the following publications, in which these poems first appeared, sometimes in slightly different versions:

Alimentum: The Literature of Food: "Farmer's Market"
Angle: "Dance of a Dozen Lovers," "Bee Bouts-rimés," "Birdhouse," and "Sonett"
Chiron Review: "When I Meet Her By the Seashore"
Chronicles: "The Acrobats"
Eclectica: "Soup" and "Facts About Romance"
Harrington Lesbian Literary Quarterly: "Wu Tsao's Seclusion"
Journal of Lesbian Studies: "A Cappella"
Light Quarterly: "How Like You This," "Red Kiss," "Sappho in Exile," "Valentine," "My Rhona," "Lingua Lesbian," "Open Sea," "Workshop Romance," "Stationmaster," "Ladies in Waiting," "What We Do," "Prayer for Leaf," "Trip Triolet 1." (as "The Duchess of Dishes") and "Trip Triolet 3." (as "Trip Triolet")
Mezzo Cammin: "Beginning with a Line by Robert Frost"
Poetry Northeast: "I wanted you"
Rattle: "The Romance of Middle Age"
Rhythm Poetry Magazine: "Lone Poem"
Sentence: A Journal of Prose Poetics: "Eureka Springs"
Sinister Wisdom: "may the women in prison dance"
Sixty-Six: The Journal of Sonnet Studies: "On the Breakwater" and "The Loser's Lament"
Snakeskin: "Charlotte Mew," "Daylight Losing Time," "Elaine," and "Trip Triolet 2." (as "Haircut by Angelo (Capelli D'Angelo)")
SN Review: "What will I do?," "The Boston Soak," and "Intersection"

Sugar Mule: "Had We But," "And," and "Time"
The Barefoot Muse: "I'm still here"
The Gay & Lesbian Review: "Gaze"
The Labletter: "Beginning to Dance"
The Lyric: "On the 40th Anniversary of Lillian & Phyllis" (as "Portrait of a Lady")
The Spectator: "The Great God Pollen"
Tilt-a-Whirl: "What rhymes with breasts?"
Verse Wisconsin: "To Be Recited On The Fourth Plinth In Trafalgar Square"
Writers Among Artists: "Vincent Van Go-Gogh"

Thanks also to the editors who reprinted these poems:

A Gay & Gray Anthology (New Town Writers Chicago, 2011): "The Romance of Middle Age" and "Wu Tsao's Seclusion"
American Life in Poetry, Per Contra, the Poetry Foundation, and *The New York Times:* "The Romance of Middle Age"
Journal of Lesbian Studies: "Gaze"
Lady Business (Sibling Rivalry Press, 2012): "Farmer's Market," "When I Meet Her By the Seashore," "My Rhona," and "Hot Spell"
Lilt and *Rondeau Roundup:* "Red Kiss"
Sinister Wisdom: "Prayer for Leaf" and "When I Meet Her By the Seashore"
Sixty-Six: The Journal of Sonnet Studies: "The Great God Pollen"
Street Spirit: "Stationmaster," "Prayer for Leaf," and "Red Kiss"
The Bloomsbury Anthology of Jewish American Poetry (Bloomsbury Publishing, 2013): "The Romance of Middle Age" and "I'm still here"

Made in the USA
Charleston, SC
22 September 2014